100+ Halloween Jokes

Johnny B. Laughing

DEDICATION

This book is dedicated to everyone that loves a funny joke. Laughter is one of the best gifts you can give. It always puts a smile on your face, warms your heart, and makes you feel great.

CONTENTS

FUNNY HALLOWEEN JOKES

Q: What does a vampire take for a cold?

A: Coffin syrup!

Q: Did you hear about the ghost comedian?

A: He was booed off stage!

Q: What does a polite monster say when he meets you for the first time?

A: Pleased to eat you!

Q: What happened to the two mad vampires?

A: They both went a little batty!

Q: What did the werewolf write at the bottom of the letter?

A: Best vicious!

Q: Who won the Monster Beauty Contest?

A: No one!

Q: Which day of the week do ghosts like best?

A: Moandays!

Q: What has webbed feet and fangs?

A: Count Quackula!

Q: What does a monster do when he loses his head?

A: He calls the head hunter!

Q: How do warty witches keep their hair in place?

A: Scare spray!

Q: What do vampires cross the sea in?

A: Blood vessels!

Q: What do ghosts drink the most?

A: Ghoul-aid!

Q: On which day do monsters eat people?

A: Chewsday!

Q: What happened to the witch with an upside down nose?

A: Every time she sneezed her hat blew off!

Q: Why did the vampire take up acting?

A: It was in his blood!

Q: What do ghosts drink in the morning?

A: Coffee with scream and sugar!

Q: What do you call two witches who share a room?

A: Broom-mates!

Q: Where is Dracula's office?

A: The Vampire State Building!

Q: How do you stop a monster digging up your garden?

A: Take his shovel away!

Q: What happened to the naughty witch at school?

A: She was ex-spelled!

Q: When do vampires bite you?

A: Wincedays!

Q: How did the beautician style the ghost's hair?

A: With a scare dryer!

Q: What does a monster mom say to her kids at dinnertime?

A: Do not talk with someone in your mouth!

Q: Have you heard about the good weather witch?

A: She's forecasting sunny spells!

Q: What is the first thing that vampires learn at school?

A: The alphabat!

Q: What city is a ghost's favorite?

A: Mali-Boo!

Q: Why was the witch so bad at English?

A: Because wasn't very good at spelling!

Q: What is Dracula's favorite ice cream flavor?

A: Vein-illa!

Q: What happens if a big hairy monster sits in front of you at the movie theater?

A: You will miss most of the film.

Q: What happens when you see twin witches?

A: You won't be able to tell which witch is which!

Q: Why was the young vampire a failure?

A: Because he fainted at the sight of blood!

Q: How do ghosts fly from one place to another?

A: On a scareplane!

Q: How do man-eating monsters count to a thousand?

A: On their warts!

Q: How do witches lose weight?

A: They join weight witches!

Q: Why wouldn't the vampire eat his soup?

A: Because it clotted!

Q: How does a ghost start a letter?

A: Tomb it may concern!

Q: Did you hear about the girl monster who wasn't pretty and wasn't ugly?

A: She was pretty ugly!

Q: How can you tell when witches are carrying a time bomb?

A: You can hear their brooms tick!

Q: Who is a vampire likely to fall in love with?

A: The girl necks door!

Q: What does the hungry monster get after he has eaten too much ice cream?

A: More ice cream!

Q: What does a vampire stand on after taking a shower?

A: A bat mat!

Q: How can you make a witch itch?

A: Take away her W!

Q: Where do baby ghosts go during the day?

A: Day-scare centers!

Q: What did the big, hairy monster do when he lost a hand?

A: He went to the second-hand shop!

Q: What is a vampire's favorite sport?

A: Batminton!

Q: How do you picture yourself flying on a broom?

A: By witchful thinking!

Q: What is a vampire's favorite soup?

A: Scream of mushroom!

Q: What do ghosts watch if they want to relax?

A: Skelly-vision!

Q: Why was the monster standing on his head?

A: He was turning things over in his mind!

Q: Did you hear about the vampire who died of a broken heart?

A: He had loved in vein!

Q: What would you get if you crossed a witch with a famous movie director?

A: Steven Spellberg!

Q: What did the mother ghost say to the naughty baby ghost?

A: Spook when your spooken to!

Q: Why did the monster take his nose apart?

A: He wanted to see what made it run!

Q: Did you hear about the vampire who got married?

A: He proposed to his goul-friend!

Q: Where do ghosts get their mail?

A: At the ghost office!

Q: What is Dracula's favorite fruit?

A: Neck-tarines!

Q: What does an Australian witch ride on?

A: A broomerang!

Q: What should you do if a monster runs through your front door?

A: Run through the back door!

Q: Why did the vampire have pedestrian eyes?

A: They looked both ways before they crossed!

Q: Who did the ghost invite to his party?

A: Anyone he could dig up!

Q: How does a girl vampire flirt?

A: She bats her eyes!

Q: What is the best way of stopping infection from witch bites?

A: Don't bite any witches!

Q: What kind of monster is safe to put in the washing machine?

A: A wash-n-wear wolf!

Q: Why was the vampire thought of as simple-minded?

A: Because he was a complete sucker!

Q: What do young female monsters do at parties?

A: They go around looking for edible bachelors!

Q: Why did the vampire attack the clown?

A: He wanted the circus to be in his blood!

Q: What did the young witch say to her mother?

A: Can I have the keys to the broom tonight?

Q: How do you join a Vampire Fan Club?

A: Send your name, address and blood type!

Q: Which ghost ate too much porridge?

A: Ghouldilocks.

Q: Did you hear about the vampire who had an eye for the ladies?

A: He used to keep it in his back pocket!

Q: What can a monster do that you can't do?

A: Count up to 25 on his fingers!

Q: What is a vampire's favorite hobby?

A: In-grave-ing!

Q: Why is stupid monster like a jack-o-lantern?

A: They both have empty heads!

Q: Why does Dracula always travel with his coffin?

A: Because his life is at stake!

Q: What European capital has the most ghosts?

A: Boodapest!

Q: What is a monster's favorite play to watch?

A: Romeo and Ghouliet!

Q: What kind of witch goes to the beach?

A: A sandwitch!

Q: What do vampires have at eleven o'clock every day?

A: A coffin break!

Q: How does a monster begin a fairy tale?

A: Once upon a slime there was...

Q: When do ghosts play tricks on each other?

A: On April Ghouls Day!

Q: What happened to Ray when he met the man-eating monster?

A: He became an ex-Ray!

Q: How does Dracula like to have his food served?

A: In bite-sized pieces!

Q: What do ghosts use to phone home?

A: A terror-phone!

Q: What monster plays the most April Fools jokes on others?

A: Prankenstein!

Q: What kind of street does a ghost like best?

A: A dead end!

Q: What is the hardest thing about making monster soup?

A: Stirring it!

Q: What do you get if you cross Dracula with Al Capone?

A: A fangster!

Q: How did skeletons send each other letters in the days of the Wild West?

A: Bony Express!

Q: Why did the monster get a ticket at Thanksgiving dinner?

A: He was exceeding the feed limit!

Q: What is a witch's favorite TV show?

A: Lifestyles of the Witch and Famous!

Q: What did the little ghost eat for lunch?

A: A booloney sandwich!

Q: What do they have for lunch at Monster School?

A: Human beans, boiled legs, and eyes-cream!

Q: Why did Dracula go to the dentist?

A: He wanted to improve his bite!

Q: What does a zombie say when he gets a letter from his goulfriend?

A: It's a dead letter day!

Q: What do sea monsters have for dinner?

A: Fish and ships!

Q: Why is a ghost like an empty house?

A: Because there's no body there!

Q: What's the favorite subject of young witches at school?

A: Spelling!

Q: How do you stop a monster from smelling?

A: Cut off his nose!

Q: What is Dracula's favorite pudding?

A: Leeches and scream!

Q: What do you get if you cross a monster with a flea?

A: Lots of very scared dogs!

Q: Why don't ghosts make good magicians?

A: You can see right through their tricks!

Q: Why does Dracula have no friends?

A: Because he's a pain in the neck!

FIND THE DIFFERENCES

MAZE #1

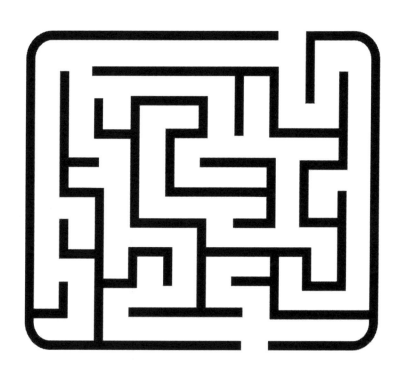

MAZE #2

MAZE #3

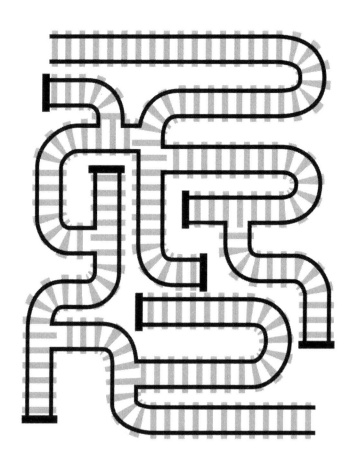

MAZE #4

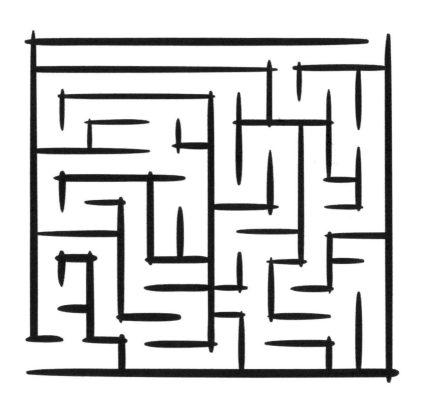

MAZE #5

MAZE #6

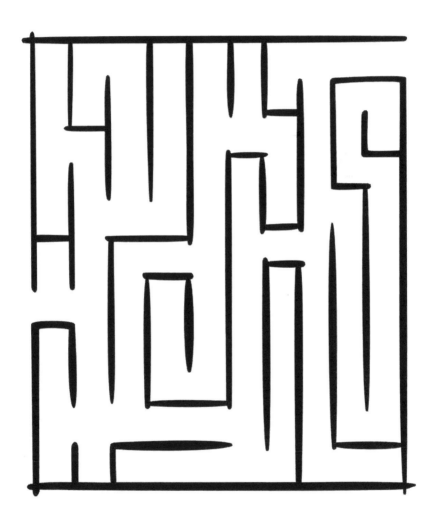

MAZE #7

MAZE #8

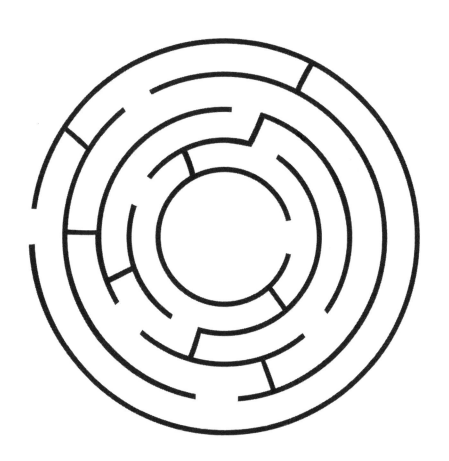

FIND THE DIFFERENCE SOLUTION

MAZE SOLUTIONS 1-4

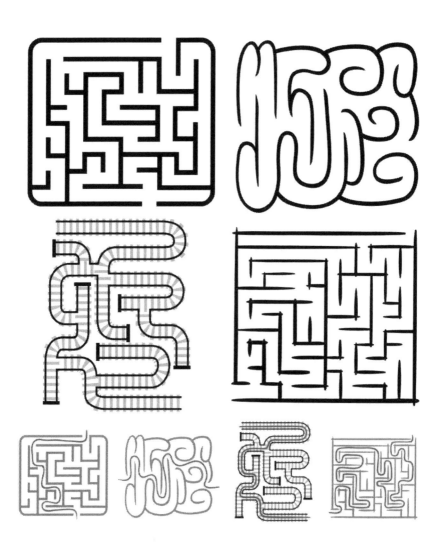

MAZE SOLUTIONS 5-8

ABOUT THE AUTHOR

The Joke King, Johnny B. Laughing is a best-selling children's joke book author. He is a jokester at heart and enjoys a good laugh, pulling pranks on his friends, and telling funny and hilarious jokes!

For more funny joke books just search for
JOHNNY B. LAUGHING on Amazon

-or-

Visit the website:
www.funny-jokes-online.weebly.com

Made in the USA
San Bernardino, CA
23 October 2018